Yuuyaraq
The Way of the Human Being

by

Harold Napoleon

with commentary

edited by Eric Madsen

ALASKA NATIVE KNOWLEDGE NETWORK

Printed in the United States of America

Sixth Printing, August 2004

Published by the Alaska Native Knowledge Network
University of Alaska Fairbanks
Harper Building
P.O. Box 756280
Fairbanks, Alaska 99775–6280

Cover photograph courtesy of University of Alaska Museum.
Owl mask from Kashunuk (made 1946).
Now an abandoned site, Kashunuk was located about 18 miles southeast of the
village of Hooper Bay, near the mouth of the Kashunuk River.

Elmer E. Rasmuson Library Cataloging-in-Publication Data

Napoleon, Harold.

Yuuyaraq: the way of the human being / Harold Napoleon; edited by Eric
Madsen—Fairbanks : Center for Cross-Cultural Studies, University of Alaska
Fairbanks, 1991.

p. cm.

ISBN 1–877962–21–X

1. Indians of North America—Alaska—Diseases. I. Madsen, Eric. II. University of
Alaska Fairbanks. Center for Cross-Cultural Studies. II. Title.

E98.D6N36 1991

To George Napoleon II,
who loved "from here to the mountains,"
and to the unborn victims and survivors of the Great Death
and their descendents,
that they may all find their peace through love and truth
and there find their freedom.

Table of Contents

Introduction

Eric Madsen
Adjunct Assistant Professor
Center for Cross-Regional Education Programs
Chukchi Campus
University of Alaska Fairbanks

Occasionally an author takes bits and pieces of information that many people are more or less familiar with and puts them together in a way that offers new possibilities for understanding events around us. The focal paper in this volume, Harold Napoleon's *Yuuyaraq*, is such a discussion about the initial and continuing effects of the epidemics that afflicted Alaskan Natives from the 1770s through the 1940s.

When Harold informally made a handwritten version of his paper available to a few people during the summer of 1990, its impact was so powerful and its appeal was so widespread that the paper took on a life of its own and quickly circulated more widely than Harold could imagine. Although he was somewhat embarrassed that his "raw" version was reprinted in a variety of places, Harold was gratified that his ideas made sense to others and he generously shared his work with everyone who was interested, asking only thoughtful—critical, if necessary—dialogue about the ideas in return. Now, with the help of many people the College of Rural Alaska is pleased to offer Harold's approved version of his paper. As readers familiar with both versions will observe, editing may not make that much difference: what commands attention here is Harold's new way of thinking about a long-standing concern, the strength and clarity of his voice, and the depth of his appeal for Native people to talk about, and thus eventually alleviate, that part of their pain he sees as having originated in the trauma following the Great Death.

That talk will not come easily. Harold suggests that *nallunguarluku*, literally, "pretending it didn't happen," has become something of a cultural trait, one manifestation of which is difficulty in talking about painful circumstances. This, he points out, can lead to alienation, anger, and self-destructive behavior that some people seek to numb with alcohol.

Did the survivors of the Great Death suffer from post traumatic stress syndrome? Some readers have asked if the diagnosis is clinically correct, or if we can even know one way or the other at this temporal distance. Harold suggests (in private conversation) that for every argument one could advance that the survivors did not suffer clinical PTSS, a reasonable argument could be made that they could not have avoided suffering many of the symptoms to which we have only recently applied that name. Other readers might wonder which of the many epidemics was actually the most traumatic. For example, Dr. Robert Fortuine, in *Chills and Fever*, indicates that "two of these epidemics, smallpox in 1835–1840 and influenza and measles in 1900, caused such devastation that they must rank among the most significant single events in the recorded history of the peoples they affected" (1989; p. 197).

For the clinician, such questions are understandably important. But for most of us, the power in Harold's presentation is not clinical but conceptual: death on a massive scale wipes out the majority of the members of a number of interrelated societies, destroys the cultural underpinnings of those societies, and leaves psychological scars on the survivors and their descendents that continue to show effects to this day. We know the epidemics that swept rural Alaska killed elders and healers and other culture bearers along with young adults and children, all in barely imaginable numbers. We know that societies depend on passing tradition and knowledge from one generation to the next so that art and intellect can grow rather than perpetually being created anew. We know that when people are unable to comprehend and come to grips with events that seem bigger than they are, dysfunctional behavior often results. And we know that Alaska Natives suffer most of the forms of dysfunctional behavior known in other segments of our society today, sadly, in higher proportions. What Harold provides is a way of integrating this knowledge, a perspective on past events we may have let slip from memory and current events that are maddeningly devoid of coherent explanation.

Harold sincerely hoped that this volume would include reactions to his paper from some of the elders, and we are pleased that Walter Soboleff, whom Harold identifies as a "teacher and friend," agreed to share some of his thoughts here. While comments from additional elders clearly would have added much to the volume and it is unfortunate that we were unable to obtain them, their absence emphasizes one of Harold's central points: the memory of the epidemics and the individual and social trauma that followed them continues to be palpable and painful. For example, we spoke to one woman who is still perfectly lucid and who sometimes tells visitors about events from her childhood now a century past. She has suffered the grief of her children dying of old age before her and the suicides of her grandchildren with the quiet dignity and understanding that reveal the true meaning of the term "elder," yet when asked about the epidemics she said, "Too much hurt. I don't want to remember."

Harold suggests that in order for Native people to end that part of today's trauma connected with the Great Death and to advance the healing process currently underway in many communities, discussion about what happened and how people feel about it must take place on a broad scale. In private conversation with Harold, this theme becomes a heartfelt plea. Perhaps it is appropriate then that those of us who are moved by Harold's paper accept his charge of finding some way to facilitate that exchange. The topic and the pain associated with it suggest that the type of sharing Harold sees as essential will not take place at some large conference but in many small interpersonal conversations. As several contributors to this volume mention, much of the healing and taking-control must occur at the village level anyway. Nevertheless, wider efforts in support of those processes may help. For example, the elders' meetings that occur in many regions might be conducive settings for conversation about this topic to begin. Written "proceedings" of the meetings could then provide one way for regions to share the interchange with each other and with those who inevitably will be unable to attend in person. Obviously the decisions as to if, and how, discussion might take place rest with Native communities, while those of us associated with institutions that serve the those communities stand ready to help—and learn—as appropriate.

Many people helped to make this volume possible. Robert Lee, a volunteer counselor at the Fairbanks Correctional Center, helped bring

Harold's paper to our attention and assisted in arranging the initial discussions that led to this publication. Carol Barnhardt keyed in Harold's original handwritten manuscript so that he could share his thoughts with a few people who had expressed interest. Gerald Mohatt, dean of the College of Rural Alaska, agreed to support its publication from college resources. Barbara Tabbert, Sue Mitchell, and Rae Ammons Jones in the college publications center were tremendously helpful with many of the more tedious but essential tasks involved in publishing a volume. Carolyn Peter contacted a number of the contributors whose papers appear and several more who were unable to contribute in the time available. All of the contributors generously volunteered their time, energy, and ideas while knowing their work would serve primarily as contextual background. None of them expected thanks, but clearly they deserve it. Steve Jacobson of the Alaska Native Language Center at UAF lent an unseen hand by suggesting standardized spellings for the Yup'ik words that appear throughout the volume. Finally, I would like to add my personal thanks to Ray Barnhardt for conceiving this volume and then entrusting me with its execution while he was on sabbatical leave exploring new ideas and creating new opportunities for other people.

Editing can be frustrating or rewarding, sometimes both. In the present case, it has been a genuine pleasure to work with the people mentioned above, all of whom accepted the challenge of bringing a modicum of uniformity and coherence to the volume as a whole while preserving the power of the individual authors' voices. No one accepted this challenge more graciously than Harold. Thank you all.

Yuuyaraq: The Way of the Human Being

Harold Napoleon
Yup'ik
Hooper Bay, Alaska

Introduction

For the past four years I have repeatedly tried to write letters and papers addressing the problem of alcoholism and alcohol abuse among Alaska's Native people. Each time I have stopped or thrown the paper away because the picture was never complete. There was always something missing. My efforts were like an incomplete sentence.

Since the death of my son, due directly to my own abuse of and addiction to alcohol, understanding the causes of this disease has occupied much of my time here at the Fairbanks Correctional Center. This prison has been like a laboratory to me; there is no shortage of subjects to be studied, namely, Alaska Natives from all parts of the state whose own abuse of alcohol also brought them here.

From my own family and village history and the histories and backgrounds of the hundreds of young Native people I have met, I have a profile of the Native addict or abuser. While the subjects may be from different villages and tribes, in almost every case the background remains the same. So now it is possible to make fairly accurate statements as to the cause or causes of this disease which yearly takes so many lives through suicide, homicide, accidental death, disease, and heartbreak. It also helps us understand the hopelessness, the frustration, the anger, the prejudice so many people have, which tragically erupts in violence under the influence of alcohol.

The theory that Native people are somehow biologically susceptible to alcohol abuse and alcoholism may have some credence, but I have discounted it as being almost insignificant. Through my own studies of the history of Alaska Native people and the history of the abusers and alcoholics I have met here and by listening to elders, I have come to the conclusion that the primary cause of alcoholism is not physical but spiritual. And to carry this one step further, since the disease is not physical or caused by physical or biological factors, then the cure must also be of the spirit.

As to my credentials, I do not hold a master's or a doctorate, but I am a Yup'ik Eskimo and I was born into a world which no longer exists. My education began in my village of Hooper Bay. I did not begin to learn English until I went to school at six years of age. I then was sent at age twelve to Copper Valley School, supposedly because the school in my village could not teach me what I needed to know.

I love to read. From the first day that I learned the alphabet and acquired a dictionary, I have read everything I could get my hands on. I ruined my eyes reading. The whole world opened up to me and I drank it in thirstily. I do not wish to boast, but I think I know the English language as well as if not better than most English speakers. I learned it from books. I am also fluent in and think in my Native tongue.

I graduated from St. Mary's High School in May 1968 and was valedictorian of my class. Thereafter I went to Great Falls, Montana, for my first year of university where I chose to study history. From there I transferred to the University of Alaska where I also studied history. In 1972 I became executive director of the Association of Village Council Presidents and in that capacity got to know more intimately my own Yup'ik people. All I had to offer them was ideas and I never tired of presenting these. The germ of freedom and self-government was introduced to them then and, happily, today they still seek independence and self-government. I was 22, I was tireless, and I fell in love with them. Soon their problems became mine. Naively, I thought I could solve them all, but needless to say, I did not.

I helped house them, clothe them, feed them, educate them, and protect their rights. I lobbied on their behalf and fought tooth and nail for them. But I now see I failed to look to the most critical part of our existence—our spiritual well being.

When I first started to work for our villages I did not drink; I did not like to drink—I didn't even like the taste. But after five years of countless meetings in Anchorage, Juneau and Washington, being with others for whom drinking was a part of their lives, like so many other Native people, I soon became addicted. But I did not know this; it just became a part of my life.

Perhaps I took myself and my responsibility too seriously, but it was what I perceived to be my failures and the subsequent frustration and anger that led to my becoming an alcoholic. I was too young, too inexperienced, and I took everything to heart. But something in my soul, in my background, my family's and village's history, had preconditioned me to internalize and personalize every perceived defeat.

This is not to say I did no good. Certainly I must have, because in many ways, I left our people in better shape than when they gave me so much responsibility at age twenty-two. I gave them my best, and so did my family. We sacrificed a great deal for them. I was hardly home but my children had to stay home waiting for me. Yes, I gave my best and my children gave me, their father, to others.

My whole adult life has been spent working for our Yup'ik people; I have had no other employer but them. I have been their executive director, vice-president, president and vice-chairman. This is my history until June of 1984 when my world, as I knew it then, ended with the death of my son.

I am now 39 years of age at the writing of this paper. The first 21 years of my life I was in school, and the next 13 years I spent working for our Yup'ik people. The last five years I have spent in prison as a direct result of my alcoholism. These last five years I have spent grieving, not only for my son, but for all the others who have died in this long night of our alcohol-induced suffering. I have also spent that time looking into my own soul and the souls of my fellow Native people who have become afflicted with this disease.

It is a disease because the people who suffer from it do not volunteer to become infected. No one volunteers to live a life of misery, sorrow, disappointment, and hopelessness. No one in his right mind chooses to lose a loved one, to break his family's heart, to go to prison. It is a disease because no one will beat his wife, molest his children, or give them little rest, because he wants to. No man dreams of this. Yet sadly, this is what is happening too often in our villages and in our homes, and we have to stop it. We have to arrest this disease, this unhappiness, this suffering, and the good news is that we can.

This paper tries to deal with the causes of alcoholism and alcohol abuse among this generation of Alaska Native people. It is not intended to be a history or a study of the cultures of the various tribes. But because of the nature of the subject, pertinent aspects of the old Yup'ik culture will be briefly discussed so as to give the reader some background and a better understanding of the subject. Things don't just happen; there are causes and reasons, and if we try to understand these causes and reasons, then conceivably we will know how to better deal with the problem.

Although I am an Alaska Native, I am first a Yup'ik, and it is from this perspective that I think and write. However, I have found so many similarities among the important cultural aspects of the various tribes that it would be safe to say that we are, in fact, one tribe of many families.

Yuuyaraq

Prior to the arrival of Western people, the Yup'ik were alone in their riverine and Bering Sea homeland—they and the spirit beings that made things the way they were. Within this homeland they were free and secure. They were ruled by the customs, traditions, and spiritual beliefs of their people, and shaped by these and their environment: the tundra, the river and the Bering Sea.

Their world was complete; it was a very old world. They called it Yuuyaraq, "the way of being a human being." Although unwritten, this way can be compared to Mosaic law because it governed all aspects of a human being's life. It defined the correct behavior between parents and children, grandparents and grandchildren, mothers-in-law and daughters and sons-in-law. It defined the correct behavior between cousins (there were many cousins living together in a village). It determined which members of the community could talk with each other and which members could tease each other. It defined acceptable behavior for all members of the community. It outlined the protocol for every and any situation that human beings might find themselves in.

Yuuyaraq defined the correct way of thinking and speaking about all living things, especially the great sea and land mammals on which the Yup'ik relied for food, clothing, shelter, tools, kayaks, and other essentials. These great creatures were sensitive; they were able to understand human conversations, and they demanded and received respect. *Yuuyaraq* prescribed the correct method of hunting and fishing and the correct way of handling all fish and game caught by the hunter in order to honor and appease their spirits and maintain a harmonious relationship with them.

Yuuyaraq encompassed the spirit world in which the Yup'ik lived. It outlined the way of living in harmony within this spirit world and with the spirit beings that inhabited this world. To the Yup'ik, the land, the rivers, the heavens, the seas, and all that dwelled within them were spirit, and therefore sacred. They were born not only to the physical world of the Bering Sea, the Yukon, and the Kuskokwim rivers, but into a spirit world as well. Their arts, tools, weapons, kayaks and umiaks, songs and dances, customs and traditions, thoughts and actions—all bore the imprint of the spirit world and the spirit beings.

When the Yup'ik walked out into the tundra or launched their kayaks into the river or the Bering Sea, they entered into the spiritual realm. They lived in deference to this spiritual universe, of which they were, perhaps, the weakest members. *Yuuyaraq* outlined for the Yup'ik the way of living in this spiritual universe. It was the law by which they lived.

The Spirit World

To the Western explorers, whalers, traders, and missionaries who first met them, the Yup'ik were considered backward savages steeped in superstition. Their villages were small and hard to find because they were a part of the earth. Grass grew on their houses, making it hard to see the village. Only when the warriors came out in their kayaks and umiaks did the newcomers see them and then they were surprised that humans would already be in this part of the world.

The river banks were red with fish drying on racks, along with seal, walrus, and whale meat. Women and children were everywhere, curious and afraid. The old men were curious but unafraid, their interest piqued by these white men who came on winged wooden ships.

They could not communicate by tongue so they tried to converse by signs. The white men gave the Eskimo scouts small gifts. The Yup'ik soon saw that these whites seemed friendly so they allowed them into their villages although the newcomers did not want to eat when offered food. The visitors saw the semi-subterranean sod houses with underground entrances and they smelled the stench from within. They saw the oily, unwashed faces and the tangled hair. They saw the worn skin clothes and smelled the seal oil. They saw the labrets, the nose bones, the beauty marks on the women, and the fierce, proud faces of the men. Then they were invited to a night of dancing. There they saw the wooden masks worn by the men during their dances. They felt the beating of the drums and were carried away by the singers, drummers, and dancers.

To the explorer or missionary witnessing the dancing in a dimly lit, crowded, stiflingly hot *qasgiq* (men's house), the men, stripped of their clothing, and the women, dancing naked to the waist, must have seemed like heathen savages. The *kass'aqs* (white men) thought they were witnessing a form of devil worship and might even have been frightened by it. The white men did not understand what they were seeing. They did not know that for a brief time they had entered the spirit world of the Yup'ik Eskimo.

To the Yupiit, the world visible to the eye and available to the senses showed only one aspect of being. Unseen was the spirit world, a world just as important as the visible, if not more so. In fact, Yup'ik life was lived in deference to this world and the spirit beings that inhabited it.

What the white men saw was not worship of the devil, but a people paying attention—being mindful of the spirit beings of their world with whom they had to live in harmony. They knew that the temporal and the spiritual were intertwined and they needed to maintain a balance between the two. The Westerners had witnessed the physical representation of that spirit world as presented by dance, song, and mask. But they did not understand what they were seeing; they were strangers in the spirit world of the Bering Sea Eskimo.

Iinruq

The Yup'ik word for spirit is *iinruq*. The Yup'ik believed that all things, animate and inanimate, had *iinruq*. *Iinruq* was the essence, the soul, of the object or being. Hence, a caribou was a caribou only because it possessed a caribou *iinruq*, a caribou spirit.

Iinruq were indestructible, unlike the bodies in which they resided. And in the case of men, fish, and game, death was the spirit leaving the body. This is why the Yup'ik prescribed respectful ways of treating even dead animals. They believed the *iinruq* would, in time, take another body and come back, and if it had been treated with respect, it would be happy to give itself to the hunter again. For a people solely dependent on sea and land mammals, fish, and waterfowl for subsistence, it was imperative that all members of the community treat all animals with respect or face starvation as a result of an offended spirit. For this reason, annual feasts were held to celebrate and appease the spirits of the animals the village had caught during that year. Some white men witnessed such feasts.

The Russian naval officer L. A. Zagoskin and the American ethnographer Edward W. Nelson witnessed the Bladder Feast. They called it that because the center of attention seemed to be the bladders of sea mammals hanging in the center of the *qasgiq*. Hanging with the bladders were spears, throwing darts, bows and arrows—all the hunting implements of the hunters. Both observers were moved by the dancing, the oratory they did not understand, and the ritual. But what they did not understand was the unseen— the spirits represented by the bladders.

Not only the animals possessed *iinruq*, humans also possessed them. But human spirits were not called *iinruq*. In the Hooper Bay dialect, they are called *anerneq*—literally, "breath"—and as in animals, a human being could not live without its breath. Death came when the *anerneq* left the body due to injury, illness, or by the will of the person. The human spirit was a very powerful spirit and, like the spirits of other living creatures, was reborn when its name was given to a newborn. These spirits were appeased and celebrated through the Great Feast of the Dead, as Nelson called it.

Even so, animal and human spirits wandered the earth, as did monsters and creatures of the deep and the underground, good spirits and evil spirits (*alangrut*) that either helped or caused havoc, even death, for humans and animals alike. Every physical mani-festation—plenty of food or famine, good weather or bad, good luck or bad, health or illness—had a spiritual cause. This is why the shamans, the *angalkuq*, were the most important men and women in the village.

The *angalkuq* were the village historians, physicians, judges, arbitrators, and interpreters of *Yuuyaraq*. They also understood the spirit world and at times entered into it to commune with the spirit beings in fulfillment of their responsibility as intermediaries between humans and the spiritual realm. *Angalkuq* are said to have gone to the moon, to the bottom of the sea, and to the bowels of the earth in their search for understanding and solutions to problems which faced their people, such as famine, bad weather, and illness.

In the old Yup'ik world, the *angalkuq* were powerful and indispensable forces because they represented, protected, and upheld *Yuuyaraq*, even against the spiritual realm, of which they were members. They were the guardians of an ancient culture that had become brittle with age, a culture whose underpinnings the rest of the world would never understand, a culture that was about to crumble as a result of temporal forces from the one direction the *angalkuq* were not looking—the physical world.

Illness and Disease

Not knowing of microbes, bacteria, or viruses, the old Yup'ik attributed illness to the invasion of the body by evil spirits. They knew that certain plants and spoiled food caused death and they strictly forbade the eating of them. But illness unattributed to the ingestion of poisons through the mouth was attributed to evil spirits. Such illness was treated by the *angalkuq* in their role as medicine men and women.

Certain herbs, plants, and even animal parts provided commonly known remedies for many ailments suffered by the Yup'ik. They also had home remedies for small burns and cuts, sore backs, sprains, and other minor ailments. The *angalkuq* were not called in unless the illness was deemed to be serious and of an unknown nature, probably caused by an evil spirit and thus requiring a spiritual remedy.

The *angalkuq* must have known that some of the ailments were, by nature, physical. Their knowledge of the human anatomy was probably as good as that of their Western counterparts at that time. Some *angalkuq* were even said to have performed surgeries, amputations, and autopsies. They had names for all major bones, muscles, arteries, veins, and organs, and knew roughly the function of each. But their remedies for unknown disease were different from their Western counterparts who used bromides and elixirs, while the *angalkuq* used songs, dances, and chants.

The important thing to remember is that the old Yupiit believed that illnesses unattributed to the ingestion of poisons or injury were caused by the invasion of the body by evil spirits. With the arrival of Western man, the Yupiit (and *Yuuyaraq*) would be accosted by diseases from which they would never recover. The old Yup'ik culture, the spirit world and its guardian, the *angalkuq*, were about to receive a fatal wounding.

The World Goes Upside Down

When the first white men arrived in the Yup'ik villages, the people did not immediately abandon their old ways. It is historical fact that they resisted Russian efforts to colonize them. They did not abandon their spirit world or their beliefs upon first hearing the Christian message of the priests. That the missionaries met resistance is clear from the derogatory and antagonistic references they made about the *angalkuq* in their diaries. They called them rascals, tricksters, even agents of the devil.

The Yupiit saw missionaries as curiosities, as they saw all white men. The Yupiit said of them, *yuunritut,*—"they are not human beings." Obviously they were not impressed by the white men, even though they quickly adopted their technology and goods. But resistance to Western rule would crumble, *Yuuyaraq* would be abandoned, and the spirit world would be displaced by Christianity.

The change was brought about as a result of the introduction of diseases that had been born in the slums of Europe during the dark and middle ages, diseases carried by the traders, the whalers, and the missionaries. To these diseases the Yup'ik and other

Native tribes had no immunity, and to these they would lose up to 60 percent of their people. As a result of epidemics, the Yup'ik world would go upside down; it would end.

This period of Yup'ik history is vague. There is no oral or written record of their reaction to this experience, but we can and must attempt in our minds to recreate what happened because this cataclysm of mass death changed the persona, the lifeview, the world view, of the Yup'ik people.

The Great Death

As a child I heard references to *yuut tuqurpallratni*—"when a great many died," or The Great Death. I never understood when it happened, nor was I told in detail what it was. But I learned that it was a time-mark for our Yup'ik people and that it was caused by disease.

I heard references to *yuut tuqurpallratni* from three men, my granduncles, all of whom are now dead. Their white man-given names were Joe Seton, Frank Smart, and Sam Hill, but of course we did not call them that. To me they were my *Apakcuaq*, my *Apaiyaq*, and my *Angakalaq*. In almost every reference to the experience, they used the word *naklurluq*, or "poor," referring both to the dead and to the survivors, but they never went into detail. It was almost as if they had an aversion to it.

From looking at the various epidemics which decimated the Native people, I at first thought of them collectively as the Great Death, but I am now convinced that the Great Death referred to the 1900 influenza epidemic which originated in Nome. From there it spread like a wildfire to all corners of Alaska, killing up to 60 percent of the Eskimo and Athabascan people with the least exposure to the white man. (Details are reported by Robert Fortuine in his book, *Chills and Fever*). This epidemic killed whole families and wiped out whole villages. It gave birth to a generation of orphans—our current grandparents and great-grandparents.

The suffering, the despair, the heartbreak, the desperation, and confusion these survivors lived through is unimaginable. People watched helplessly as their mothers, fathers, brothers, and sisters grew ill, the efforts of the *angalkuq* failing. First one family fell ill, then another, then another. The people grew desperate, the angalkuq along with them. Then the death started, with people wailing morning, noon, and night. Soon whole families were dead, some leaving only a boy or girl. Babies tried to suckle on the breasts of dead mothers, soon to die themselves. Even the medicine men grew ill and died in despair with their people, and with them died a great part of *Yuuyaraq*, the ancient spirit world of the Eskimo.

The Survivors

Whether the survivors knew or understood, they had witnessed the fatal wounding of *Yuuyaraq* and the old Yup'ik culture. Compared to the span of life of a culture, the Great Death was instantaneous. The Yup'ik world was turned upside down, literally overnight. Out of the suffering, confusion, desperation, heartbreak, and trauma was born a new generation of Yup'ik people. They were born into shock. They woke to a world in shambles, many of their people and their beliefs strewn around them, dead. In their minds they had been overcome by evil. Their medicines and their medicine men and women had proven useless. Everything they had believed in had failed. Their ancient world had collapsed.

From their innocence and from their inability to understand and dispel the disease, guilt was born into them. They had witnessed mass death—evil—in unimaginable and unacceptable terms. These were the men and women orphaned by the sudden and traumatic death of the culture that had given them birth. They would become the first generation of modern-day Yup'ik.

The Survivors' World

The world the survivors woke to was without anchor. The *angalkuq*, their medicines, and their beliefs, had all passed away overnight. They woke up in shock, listless, confused, bewildered, heartbroken, and afraid. Like soldiers on an especially gruesome battlefield, they were shell shocked.

Too weak to bury all the dead, many survivors abandoned the old villages, some caving in their houses with the dead still in them. Their homeland—the tundra, the Bering Sea coast, the riverbanks—had become a dying field for the Yup'ik people:

families, leaders, artists, medicine men and women—and *Yuuyaraq*. But it would not end there.

Famine, starvation, and disease resulting from the epidemic continued to plague them through the 1950s, and many more perished. These were the people whom the missionaries would call wretched, lazy, even listless. Gone were the people whom Nelson so admired for their "arts, ingenuity, perseverance and virtuosity," the people whom Henry B. Collins claimed had reached the "peak" of modern Eskimo art. Disease had wiped them out. The long night of suffering had begun for the survivors of the Great Death and their descendants.

The End of the Old Culture
The Yup'ik people of today are not culturally the same as their forebears. They are, however, linked to the old through the experience of the Great Death. One was wiped out by it, the other was born out of it and was shaped by it. It is from this context that we have to see the modern Yup'ik Eskimo. It is only from this context that we can begin to understand them.

Like any victim or witness of evil, whether it be murder, suicide, rape, war or mass death, the Yup'ik survivors were in shock. But unlike today's trauma victims, they received no physical or psychological help. They experienced the Great Death alone in the isolation of their tundra and riverine homeland. There was no Red Cross, no relief effort. The survivors of the Great Death had to face it alone.

They were quiet and kept things to themselves. They rarely showed their sorrows, fears, heartbreak, anger, or grief. Unable to relive in their conscious minds the horror they had experienced, they did not talk about it with anyone. The survivors seem to have agreed, without discussing it, that they would not talk about it. It was too painful and the implications were too great. Discussing it would have let loose emotions they may not have been able to control. It was better not to talk about it, to act as if it had never happened, to *nallunguaq*. To this day *nallunguaq* remains a way of dealing with problems or unpleasant occurrences in Yup'ik life. Young people are advised by elders to *nallunguarluku*, "to pretend it didn't happen." They had a lot to pretend not to know. After all, it was not only that their loved ones had died, they also had seen their world collapse. Everything they had lived and believed had been found wanting. They were afraid to admit that the things they had believed in might not have been true.

Traumatized, leaderless, confused, and afraid, the survivors readily followed the white missionaries and school teachers, who quickly attained a status once held only by the *angalkuq*. The survivors embraced Christianity, abandoned *Yuuyaraq*, discarded their spirit world and their ceremonies, and buried their old culture in the silence of denial.

Having silently abandoned their own beliefs, the survivors were reinforced in their decision not to talk about them by the missionaries who told them their old beliefs were evil and from the *tuunraq*, "the devil." They learned to sternly tell their grandchildren not to ask them questions about the *angalkuq*, the old symbol of Yup'ik spiritualism, as if they were ashamed of them and of their old beliefs. They would become good Christians—humble, compliant, obedient, deferential, repentant, and quiet.

The survivors were fatalists. They were not sure about the future or even the next day. They told their children to always be prepared to die because they might not even wake up in the morning. They cautioned against making long-range plans. From their own experience they knew how fleeting life was, and from the missionaries they knew how terrible the wrath of the Christian God could be. As new Christians, they learned about hell, the place where the missionaries told them most of their ancestors probably went. They feared hell. They understood fear and they understood hell.

The survivors also turned over the education and instruction of their children to the missionaries and the school teachers. They taught them very little about *Yuuyaraq*. They allowed the missionaries and the school teachers to inflict physical punishment on their children; for example, washing their children's mouths with soap if they spoke Yup'ik in school or church. Their children were forbidden, on pain of "serving in hell," from dancing or following the old ways. The parents—the survivors—allowed this. They did not protest. The children were, therefore, led to believe that the ways of their fathers and forefathers were of no value and were evil. The survivors allowed this.

The survivors taught almost nothing about the old culture to their children. It was as if they were ashamed of it, and this shame they passed on to their children by their silence and by allowing cultural atrocities to be committed against their children. The survivors also gave up all governing power of the villages to the missionaries and school teachers, whoever was most aggressive. There was no one to contest them. In some villages the priest had displaced the *angalkuq*. In some villages there was theocracy under the benevolent dictatorship of a missionary. The old guardians of *Yuuyaraq* on the other hand, the *angalkuq*, if they were still alive, had fallen into disgrace. They had become a source of shame to the village, not only because their medicine and *Yuuyaraq* had failed, but also because the missionaries now openly accused them of being agents of the devil himself and of having led their people into disaster.

In their heart of hearts the survivors wept, but they did not talk to anyone, not even their fellow survivors. It hurt too much. They felt angry, bewildered, ashamed, and guilty, but all this they kept within themselves. These survivors became the forebears of the Yup'ik people and other Alaska Native tribes of today. Their experiences before, during, and after the Great Death explain in great part the persona of their children, grandchildren, and great-grandchildren who are alive today.

Posttraumatic Stress Disorder: An Illness of the Soul
In light of recent cases of Vietnam veterans who witnessed or participated in war-related events repugnant to them, and who have subsequently been diagnosed to suffer from a psychological illness called posttraumatic stress disorder (PTSD), it is apparent to me that some of the survivors of the Great Death suffered from the same disorder.

The syndrome is born of the attempted suppression in the mind of events perceived as repugnant or evil to the individual who has witnessed or participated in these events. These events were often traumatic to the individual because they involved violence, death, and mayhem by which he was repelled and for which he felt guilt and shame. Not all veterans became infected by this illness. It was mainly the veterans who tried to suppress and ignore their experiences and the resultant feelings of guilt and shame who became ill.

Posttraumatic stress disorder can cripple a person. The act of suppressing the traumatic event, instead of expunging it from the mind through confession, serves to drive it further into the psyche or soul, where it festers and begins to color all aspects of the person's life. The person who suppresses that which is unbearable to the conscious mind is trying to ignore it, trying to pretend it isn't there. In time, and without treatment, it will destroy the person, just as any illness left untreated will in time cripple and kill the body.

Because of his guilt, the person suffering from PTSD does not like himself. He is ashamed of himself, ashamed of what he saw or participated in, and is haunted by the memory, even in sleep. He becomes withdrawn, hypervigilant, hypersensitive, and is constantly living in stress. Soon he is unable to speak truthfully with other people about himself or his feelings and becomes unable to carry on close interpersonal relationships. Living under a great deal of stress in his soul, he becomes less and less able to deal with even the minor difficulties of everyday life.

To such a person, escape from self becomes a necessity because even in sleep he finds no peace. He becomes a runner, running from his memory and from himself. He gets tired and begins to despair. In this day and age, alcohol and drugs become a readily available escape from the illness. For a time, these numb the mind and soul. Without treatment, many veterans and others who suffer from PTSD become alcohol and drug abusers. Many become addicted, and as a result lose friends, wives, families, and become isolated, exacerbating an already bad situation. Being unable to hold jobs, some become dependent on others for support. Some become criminals, further isolating themselves and further depressing an already depressed soul.

Tragically, under the influence of alcohol and drugs, the pent-up anger, guilt, shame, sorrow, frustration, and hopelessness often is vented through outbursts of violence to self and others. Such acts, which are difficult for others and even for the sufferer to understand, drive him further into the deadly vortex of guilt and shame. Family and friends who knew him before he became ill swear that he is not the same person and that they do not know him anymore.

Posttraumatic stress disorder is not a physical illness, but an infection of the soul, of the spirit. I use the word infection because the person suffering from PTSD does not volunteer to become ill and does not choose the life of unhappiness which results from it. I refer to PTSD as an infection of the soul because the disease attacks the core of the person, the spirit. The disease is born out of evil or of events perceived as evil by the person. And the nature of evil is such that it infects even the innocent, dirtying their minds and souls. Because it is infectious, it requires cleansing of the soul through confession. If PTSD sufferers do not get help, they will in time destroy themselves, leaving in their wake even more trauma and heartbreak.

Posttraumatic Stress Disorder in the Survivors of the Great Death

Not all the survivors of the Great Death suffered from posttraumatic stress disorder, but a great many did. This may explain the great thirst for liquor that whalers and other Westerners found in the Eskimos along the Bering Sea and the Arctic. It was reported by whalers and the officers of the early revenue cutters that the Eskimos craved the liquor, trading all they had for it and almost starving themselves as long as they had molasses with which to make rum.

Like the Vietnam veteran or victims and witnesses of other violent and traumatic events, these Eskimos found in liquor a narcotic which numbed their troubled minds. The reports of the whalers, the revenue cutters, and other observers confirm that the Eskimos quickly became addicted to alcohol.

The only explanation for this type of behavior is that for some reason these Eskimos were psychologically predisposed to seek relief through the narcotic effects of alcohol. And although in the case of the St. Lawrence Islanders this behavior was reported in the mid-nineteenth century, it must be remembered that they had already begun to see their world crumbling as a result of interaction with Western sailors and diseases much earlier than the Yup'ik, Inupiaq, and Athabascan people who were located farther away from established sea lanes. The St. Lawrence story was only a precursor for the tragedy that would unfold on the mainland at the turn of the century.

Judging from the abrupt changes the Yup'ik and other Native people accepted at the turn of the century, literally without a fight, one can assume that they were not themselves. No people anywhere will voluntarily discard their culture, beliefs, customs, and traditions unless they are under a great deal of stress, physically, psychologically, or spiritually. Yet for some reason, the Yup'ik people did exactly that, overnight in the span of their cultural history. There may have been pockets of resistance, but they were insignificant.

With the Yup'ik people and most Alaska Native tribes, the case can be made that resistance collapsed because of mass death, resulting from famine, illness, and the trauma that accompanied these. The case can also be made that many of the survivors of the Great Death suffered from posttraumatic stress disorder, and that it was in this condition that they surrendered and allowed their old cultures to pass away.

The survivors had been beaten by an unseen great evil (mass death) that had been unleashed in their villages, killing over half the men, women, and little children. They had witnessed the violent collapse of their world, of *Yuuyaraq*. Having barely escaped the grip of death, the survivors were shaken to the core. They staggered, dazed, confused, brutalized, and scarred, into the new world, refugees in their own land, a remnant of an ancient and proud people. The world looked the same, yet everything had changed. But the memories would remain, memories of the spirit world, the way life used to be, and memories of the horrors they had witnessed and lived through.

We who are alive today cannot begin to imagine the fear, the horror, the confusion and the desperation that gripped the villages of our forebears following the Great Death. But we have learned, through the experience of Vietnam veterans infected by PTSD, that the cries of horror and despair do not end unless they are expunged from the soul. Yes, the Yup'ik survivors cried, they wailed, and they fought with all they had, but they were not heard. They had been alone in a collapsed and dying world and many of them carried the memory, the heartbreak, the guilt, and the shame, silently with them into the grave.

But we hear them today. They cry in the hearts of their children, their grandchildren, and great-grandchildren. They cry in the hearts of the children who have inherited the symptoms of their disease of silent despairing loneliness, heartbreak, confusion, and guilt. And tragically, because the children do not understand why they feel this way, they blame themselves for this legacy from their grandparents, the survivors of the Great Death who suffered from what we now call posttraumatic stress disorder.

The Children and Grandchildren of the Survivors

At the time of the Great Death, there were white people in some of the villages, mostly missionaries and traders, but they were few in number. They witnessed the Great Death, and in many cases they did the best they could to help the Native people. Yet it would be these same people who would take advantage of the demoralized condition of the survivors to change them, to civilize them, to attempt to remake them. They, and the men and women who would follow them, had no understanding of or respect for the old cultures. They considered them satanic, and made it their mission from God to wipe them out. They considered the survivors savages and used derogatory adjectives in describing them in their letters and diaries. And because of what they had just lived through, and because of their disoriented and weakened condition, the survivors allowed these newcomers to take over their lives.

What followed was an attempt at cultural genocide. The priests and missionaries impressed on the survivors that their spirit world was of the devil and was evil. They heaped scorn on the medicine men and women and told the people they were servants of the devil. They told the survivors that their feasts, songs, dances, and masks were evil and had to be abandoned on pain of condemnation and hellfire. Many villages followed these edicts. The dances and feasts disappeared.

The priests and missionaries forbade parents from teaching their children about *Yuuyaraq* and about the spirit world. They forbade the parents and children from practicing old customs and rituals based on *Yuuyaraq*, calling them taboo. Again, the survivors obeyed and their children grew up ignorant about themselves and about their history. If the children asked about the old culture, they were told by their parents not to ask such questions, as if they were ashamed or hiding something. From listening to the priest and observing the behavior of their parents, the children would come to believe that there was something wrong with their people, some dark secret to be ashamed of.

In the schoolhouse, the children were forbidden to speak in Yup'ik. The survivors did not protest even when it was learned that the schoolteachers were washing the mouths of their children with soap for speaking their mother tongue. In the schoolhouse, the children came to believe that to be Yup'ik was shameful and that to become like white people was not only desirable but essential. The children began to look down at their own people and began to see the observances of their people as quaint, shameful, and funny. That the survivors allowed all this is testimony to the degree of their individual and collective depression, especially in regard to the treatment of their children. Had Nelson made similar decrees during the time he was visiting these same villages (1870–1875), he would have been killed. Yet after the Great Death, some villages were ruled autocratically by a single priest.

The survivors were stoic and seemed able to live under the most miserable and unbearable of conditions. They were quiet, even deferential. They did not discuss personal problems with others. If they were hurt, they kept it to themselves. If they were angry, they kept it to themselves. They were lauded as being so respectful that they avoided eye-to-eye contact with others. They were passive. Very few exhibited their emotions or discussed them.

The survivors did as they were told. They were not fighters or protesters. They almost lost everything: their cultures, their languages, their spiritual beliefs, their songs, their dances, their feasts, their lands, their independence, their pride—all their inheritances. This was their way of coping with life after the cataclysm of the Great Death. The survivors had gone into themselves and receded with their tattered lives and unbearable emotions into a deep silence. It was in this condition that they raised their children, who then learned to be like their parents— passive, silent, not expressing emotions, keeping things to themselves, and not asking too many questions.

The survivors told their children about kindness, forgiveness, and sharing, yet they were unwilling to face and discuss the problems and unpleasantness in the family or the village. They did not teach their children about *Yuuyaraq*, the spirit world, or about the old culture because it was too painful to do so. Besides, the priest said it was wrong. Those who told stories told only the harmless ones. This would become part of the persona of the survivors and their descendents. Without meaning to, the survivors drove the experience of the Great Death and the resultant trauma and emotions deep into the souls of their children, who became psychologically and emotionally handicapped and who passed these symptoms on to their children and grandchildren.

The survivors' children are the grandparents of the present day Eskimo, Indian, and Aleut. It is these traits, these symptoms of posttraumatic stress disorder, which are handicapping the present generation of Alaska Native people. Several generations of suppressed emotions, confusion, and feelings of inferiority and powerlessness now permeate even the very young.

An Anomaly

Since the early 1960s, Native people have seen their material lives improve. They are no longer hungry, they are well clothed, and they now live in comparatively warm, comfortable homes. This has largely been achieved by the anti-poverty programs which were instituted in the years before and after the Great Society. Being by and large unemployed in the cash economy, Native people benefited greatly from the civil rights and anti-poverty programs of the 1960s and 1970s.

Yet, as their physical lives have improved, the quality of their lives has deteriorated (see graph). Since the 1960s there has been a dramatic rise in alcohol abuse, alcoholism, and associated violent behaviors, which have upset family and village life and resulted in physical and psychological injury, death, and imprisonment. Something self-destructive, violent, frustrated, and angry has been set loose from within the Alaska Native people. And it is the young that are dying, going to prison, and maiming themselves. Their families, their friends, their villages say they cannot understand why. Every suicide leaves a stunned family and village. Every violent crime and every alcohol-related death elicits

Figure 1.
Lifeline of the Yup'ik people

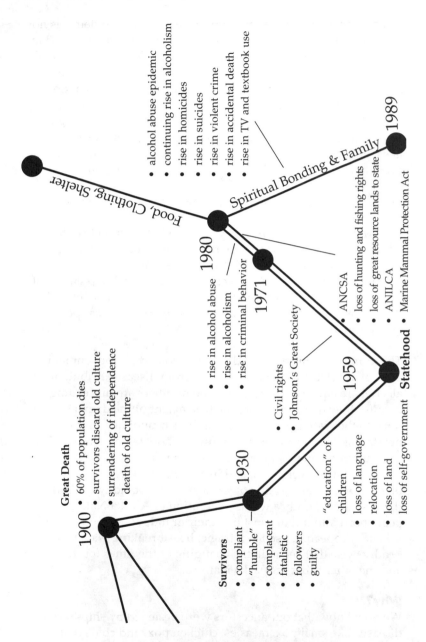

Great Death
1900
- 60% of population dies
- survivors discard old culture
- surrendering of independence
- death of old culture

Survivors
- compliant
- "humble"
- complacent
- fatalistic
- followers
- guilty

1930

- "education" of children
- loss of language
- relocation
- loss of land
- loss of self-government

- Civil rights
- Johnson's Great Society

1959

Statehood

1971

- rise in alcohol abuse
- rise in alcoholism
- rise in criminal behavior

1980

Food, Clothing, Shelter

- ANCSA
- loss of hunting and fishing rights
- loss of great resource lands to state
- ANILCA
- Marine Mammal Protection Act

- alcohol abuse epidemic
- continuing rise in alcoholism
- rise in homicides
- rise in suicides
- rise in violent crime
- rise in accidental death
- rise in TV and textbook use

Spiritual Bonding & Family

1989

the same reaction. The alcohol-related nightmare has now become an epidemic. No one seems to know why.

One thing we do know—the primary cause of the epidemic is not physical deprivation. Native people have never had it so good in terms of food, clothing, and shelter. We can also state that it isn't because the federal and state governments have ignored the problem. Hundreds of millions of dollars have been spent on Alaska Natives to improve their lives, their health, and their education. Hundreds of millions have been spent just trying to combat alcoholism and alcohol abuse among them. Local option laws have been passed that prohibit the importation, the sale, and even the possession of alcohol. Yet the carnage goes on.

The numbers are shocking. According to Matthew Berman,

> From 1977 to 1988, the last year for which complete data are available, 1,789 Native Americans died violently in Alaska. These figures include 394 deaths by suicides, 257 by homicides, and 1,138 by accident out of a total population of only 64,000 (1980 Census), representing a claim of about 3 percent of the native population over a twelve-year period (Berman 1991).

The numbers of incidents of domestic violence, imprisonments, alcohol affected children, and deaths from disease attributable to alcohol are equally shocking. Yet the numbers are misleading because they do not measure the true extent of the damage being done to the Native people. The numbers cannot quantify the heartbreak, discouragement, confusion, hopelessness, and grief. The numbers cannot measure the trauma. It is like repeating the Great Death all over again, and like then, the Alaska Natives blame themselves and do not know or understand why. And like the first Great Death, a whole generation of Alaska Natives is being born into trauma, just like their grandparents and parents. It is history repeating itself in a tragic, heartbreaking way. It is a deadly cycle that began in the changing of the times for the Yupiit and the other tribes of Alaska Natives.

Why?
We now know that our ancestors were besieged by ship-borne diseases like smallpox, measles, chicken pox, and colds that

culminated in the Great Death, the influenza epidemic at the turn of the century. Not knowing of microbes, they attributed these diseases to evil spirits and to their own weaknesses. They blamed themselves and their way of life, and abandoned themselves and their way of life as a result. But that did not end the suffering. Famine, poverty, confusion, polio, tuberculosis, and spiritual depression followed, ending in the death of the old cultures around the 1950s.

The present epidemic is a little harder to explain, but certainly it was born out of the Great Death itself, and the disease is one of the soul and the psyche of this present generation of Alaska Native people. It is an inherited disease, passed from parent to child. But it has been passed down unintentionally, unknowingly, and innocently. Nevertheless, it is deadly and unless treated, it will give birth to another generation of infected souls.

The cry of the survivors of the Great Death was why. That same cry is now heard from the confused, shocked, and heartbroken hearts of today's Alaska Native people.

A Generation Turns on Itself

Many of today's generation of Alaska Natives have turned on themselves. They blame themselves for being unemployed, for being second-class citizens, for not being successful as success is portrayed to them by the world they live in. They measure themselves by the standards of the television America and the textbook America, and they have failed. For this they blame themselves. There is no one to tell them that they are not to blame, that there is nothing wrong with them, that they are loved. Sometimes they don't even know who they are, or what they are.

This, of course, does not describe all young Alaska Native people. But it describes the suicides, the alcohol abusers, the ones in prison, the ones with nothing to do in the villages. These are the numbers we hear in reports. They are living human beings—Eskimos, Aleuts, and Indians—the ones we pay no attention to until they become numbers. Chances are that their parents also were alcohol abusers, if not alcoholics. Chances are that they were disappointed, emotionally hurt, heartbroken children. Chances are they saw physical, verbal, and psychological violence in the home. Chances are that they were not given enough attention and thought themselves unloved and unwanted. Chances are they were hungry, were dirty, were tired, and were unsuccessful in school. Chances are they yearned for happiness and a normal home but were denied it. And now, chances are they no longer communicate with others—not their parents, not their relatives, not their friends, or anyone else.

By the time such children are grown, they are deeply depressed in their souls. They have become demoralized, discouraged, and do not think very much of themselves. Deep in their hearts they are hurt, angry, frustrated and confused. They never talk. They have turned inward.

These are the ones who, when they drink alcohol, quickly become addicted to it, psychologically first, and then physically. When under the influence, they begin to vent their anger, hurt, frustration, and confusion, seemingly out of the clear blue sky. And sadly, their outbursts are directed at themselves and those closest to them: their parents, their brothers and sisters, their friends, and members of their villages. The most tragic events are those involving a blacked-out male Eskimo, Aleut, or Indian, who, while completely out of control, vents his deadly emotions in violence and mad acts resulting in dismemberment and death, thereby leaving even more traumatized victims and witnesses.

So what causes this? Is it the young man's or young woman's fault? Or is it the fault of parents who may have been abusers and alcoholics? Or is it the fault of grandparents who did not raise their children right because they themselves were traumatized by the Great Death and felt guilty about the subsequent loss of culture, language, and independence? Whose fault is it?

Certainly the dead will be buried, the suicides buried, the assaulter and abuser jailed and charged with the appropriate crime and put away in prison for a few years or a lifetime. But there are only so many prison cells. Can we seriously be thinking of putting everyone into prison? And do we keep burying the other victims of the Great Death until not a one is left? Is this to be our way of life until the end, burying the victims of the victims?

When will all this end? How will it end? How can we end it? When can we end it? Or do we even want to end it? Have we become so callous, so hard-hearted, our spiritual senses so dulled, that we are no longer moved by all this? Is it to be as Darwin put it, the survival of the fittest? My answer at least is this: We who are also the survivors of the Great Death must end it. We must activate all our energies and resources to end it. And we must do it soon because as time goes by it will become harder and harder.

Every human life is sacred. Every Yup'ik, Inupiaq, Athabascan, Aleut, Eyak, Chugiak, Tlingit, Haida, Koniag, and Tshimsian life is sacred. We are not so many that we can endlessly absorb the trauma each tragic death inflicts on our physical and psychic body. We are too few. The question is how to stop the epidemic.

Beginnings

If we were to look at the experience of the various tribes as the experience of individuals, and if they were exhibiting the symptoms we have described and which are now so well documented, we would have to spend some time just talking to them. We would have them truthfully tell their life stories, leaving nothing out, to see what was causing these disturbances in their lives. So it is in this way that we must begin to treat this particular syndrome of the various Alaska Native villages, beginning at the personal and familial levels.

The living elders must tell all they know, tell their experiences, because theirs are the experiences of the whole village, whether the whole village is aware of them or not. The very oldest are the most important because they will be able to tell their remembrances to the whole village. They must relate the old beliefs of their people, no matter the subject. They must also relate the experiences of the epidemics, no matter how painful, because these haunt not only them, but their children and grandchildren as well. They must tell why they gave everything up, why they discarded the old ways, the old beliefs, why they allowed the culture to die. They must explain how and why they gave up governing themselves, why they allowed school teachers to wash their children's mouths with soap, why they gave up so much land. The elders must speak of all that hurts them and haunts them. They owe this to their children and to their children's children because without knowing why the descendents feel the same as their elders do.

The one fear I have is that the first survivors of the Great Death—the ones who lived in the old world, were nurtured by it, and who loved it—are now almost all gone. They are the ones in whom was born the disease that afflicts Alaska Natives today. They are the ones who felt the full brunt of the fatal wounding of their world. They are the ones who saw it, were horrified by it, and whose hearts were broken. Hearing them, we will recognize the emotions in our hearts, emotions we have long attributed to a weakness within ourselves. We would at least mourn with them, mourn together the passing of our old world. Then they and we would not be alone any more.

The children of these survivors must also speak. They are now grandparents, even great-grandparents. They must speak of their childhoods, their world, what they saw, what they perceived, what they thought, how they felt. They too must share with us their life stories, leaving nothing out, the good and the bad, because their experiences are ours, and we are their seed. We also love them.

Then the parents of this new generation must speak together, as a group, to the rest of the villages. They too must relate their life stories, their experiences, their sorrows. They must turn their hearts to their children who so love them, who so long to know them. Their experiences are ours. We are shaped by them. Then we, their children, must speak to our parents, to our grandparents if we still have them, and to our own children. We, too, must tell our story to our people, because our experience is theirs too. We must tell our feelings, our anger, our frustrations, and ask questions of our parents.

We must do this because we don't know each other anymore; we have become like strangers to each other. The old do not know or understand the young, and the young do not know or understand the old. Parents do not know their children, and the children do not know their parents. As a result of this silence, a gulf has grown between those who love and care for each other the most. It is so very sad. I have been in homes where members of the same household do not even speak to each other. I wondered how they could even stand to be in the same house together like this.

And out of this will grow more hurt, misunderstanding, and unfulfilled love. Even in the family, while surrounded by those one loves the most, a person can become isolated, a stranger even to those who love him and are closest to him. Needless to say, there will be tension, stress, and frayed nerves.

Only communication, honest communication from the heart, will break this down, because inability to share one's heart and feelings is the most deadly legacy of the Great Death. It was born out of the survivors' inability to face and speak about what they had seen and lived through. The memory was too painful, the reality too hard, the results too hard to hear.

Without knowing it, the survivors began to deal with the difficulties of life by trying to ignore them, by denying them, by not talking about them. This is the way they raised their children and their children raised us the same way. Holding things in has become a trait among our families and our people. The results have been tragic.

Over the many years of suppressed emotions, of not communicating from the heart, Native people and Native families grew apart. Somewhere along the line, something had to give. The body of the Alaska Native family, village, and tribe, being unable to withstand the stresses built up from within, began breaking down.

We have seen this breakdown since the latter 1960s. Alcohol abuse has become rampant. Violence directed at self and at others in the home has erupted. The intensity and the level of self-destruction of the Alaska Native are appalling. The only way it will end is if the built-up stresses, misunderstandings, and questions are released and satisfied by truthful dialogue from the heart. It is only through this heart-to-heart dialogue, no matter how painful or embarrassing the subject, that the deadly stresses born of trauma on top of trauma can be released. Then slowly, we can all go home again, be alone and lonesome no more, be a family and a village again.

It is time we bury the old culture, mourn those who died with it, mourn with those who survived it. It is time we buried our many dead who have died in this long night of our suffering, then go forward, lost no more. We have been wandering in a daze for the last 100 years, rocked by a succession of traumatic changes and inundations. Now we have to stop, look at ourselves, and as the New Alaska Natives we are, press on together—not alone—free of the past that haunted and disabled us, free of the ghosts that haunted our hearts, free to become what we were intended to be by God.

New Alaska Natives

Several first steps should be taken on the road to health and to freedom long lost. First on the village level, those whose hearts are with their people should institute Talking Circles, where elders, parents and the young can come together to share themselves, and where the truth can be spoken about all things communal, familial, and personal.

The circle would not be a place for debate or argument, but a place to share oneself, and one's experiences, feelings, and thoughts with the rest of the village. Patience and a love for one another is a requirement for a circle. Once a circle begins, it will grow and it will strengthen those within it. It is not only a place to get things off one's chest, but a place to reestablish bonds between family members and the rest of the village. If the circle goes well, some mothers will see their sons for the first time, some sons see their fathers for the first time, and they will love them even as understanding grows.

The circle has to be open to all members of the village. No one should ever be excluded. In fact everyone must not only be invited, but welcomed and openly received by the circle. If all goes well, the bonds between family members and village members will grow. Hopefully it will enable all members of the village family to go home again. The chasm of suffering and pain that the Great Death brought to our people will close. If this should happen, then all the suffering and those who gave their lives in this long night will not have been in vain.

Another first step is the establishment of Talking Circles specifically for members of the village who have become addicted to alcohol and other drugs. Like the circle for the village in general, this circle would help the alcoholics to understand better why they became addicted and, with the help of recovering addicts, get on the road to recovery and health. To this circle

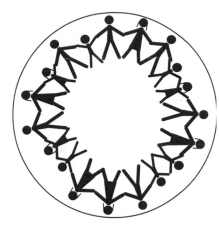

- A healthy village is a circle whose people are safe within its fold.

- Love, understanding, kindness, culture, history, goals, and truth make the circle strong and protect the village, the family, and the individual.

- A healthy village is a gift of the Creator to His children.

- For many Alaska Natives the circle was broken by the trauma of mass death through epidemics.

- Families and villages lost communication and grew apart.

- A circle broken is incomplete. It hemorrhages, and life flows out of it. It breeds unhappiness. Unless the circle is repaired in time, it will die.

- The circle can only be made whole again by those who live in it, its people.

- The circle, being spirit, can only be repaired by love, understanding, kindness, forgiveness, and patience, with the help of the Creator who established the circle. It can only be done by its people coming together in truth.

should come elders, parents, and friends who love them—to hear them, to see them, to reassure them, to receive them.

In addition to the circles, the village council should sponsor, on a regular basis, activities for the whole village that require no money but would serve to entertain and allow the families to come together as one big family, which the village is. These might be weekly potlucks with singing and dancing, perhaps even dancing classes for the bigger feasts. The village council should also reinstitute the various potlatches where the whole village can come together to celebrate their lives and the gifts they have received from their Creator.

There are a lot of things the village councils and their people can do for one another to help themselves, to bring themselves together. Even the young women could give all the mothers a night or day off by taking care of the children for one day or night so the mothers can come together as a group. There is no end to what good people in the villages can do for one another, no end to the kindnesses and small considerations they can give to each other. The important first step is for the families and the village to come together as a family. Their health and happiness depend on each other.

On Public Policies

The United States Congress has recently enacted legislation creating a commission to study the problem we have been discussing. And certainly this is one of the things Congress can do to help Native people on their road to recovery. However, it is a mistake to think that Congress or any other group can bring the Alaska Native people back to health. Money, programs, or loans, no matter how well intentioned, cannot end the unhappiness, dissatisfaction, anger, frustration, and sorrow that is now leading so many Alaska Natives to alcohol abuse, alcoholism, and tragedy. Only Alaska Natives can do this. To look elsewhere for solutions is illusory.

However, Congress can take some concrete steps to assist the Native villages in reestablishing themselves. First, Congress can affirm, by law, what is now reality: that Alaska Native people are legally Indians, and as such fall under the special protections of the U. S. Constitution and Federal Indian Law. Congress can reaffirm Alaska Natives' inherent right to self-government under whatever democratic form that government may take. It can reaffirm their right to establish tribal courts and ordinances and the power to enforce these.

Congress can reaffirm the right of Alaska Native people in the villages to hunt and fish for subsistence and give them priority rights to the economic utilization of fish and game resources so their dependence on federal welfare programs may decrease and hopefully in time, disappear. It makes no sense at all that presently many Native people are unable to hunt and fish on their lands and waters for commercial purposes while others, even foreigners, are allowed to do so, and this in an economically depressed village where there is 80 percent unemployment and where 90 percent of the families are on various welfare programs.

Congress should use some of the oil lease money it earns from lands and waters adjacent to the villages to fund scholarships for Alaska Native students studying at universities worldwide. As it is now, the benefits received by Alaska Natives come in the form of welfare payments and other grants-for-the-needy programs for which they are eligible.

Congress should also establish correctional facilities for Alaska Native offenders that would be run by Alaska Natives themselves. This would be in recognition of the fact that the village offender is not the same as the black or white offender, and that his rehabilitation can only be brought about through culturally relevant programs. These facilities should have a span of twenty years and then close at the end of that period. Congress should also appropriate funds for the establishment of substance abuse programs designed and run by Alaska Natives themselves. As with the correctional facilities, these should also have a life span of twenty years, to be closed at the end of that period.

Yes, the Congress of the United States can help the Native people on their road to recovery from the various traumas they have lived through in the past hundred years. But that help cannot come in the form of more welfare programs or programs conceived anywhere else but in the villages and by Natives themselves. The Congress of the United States is supposed to be the protector of Alaska's Native people, but for the past hundred years it has neglected them, failed to protect them, and instead has become a party to elements which would completely disenfranchise them as a people.

Yes, the Congress and the American people can help the Eskimos, Aleuts, and Indians to become free, self-supporting Americans, but they must realize that Native people can only do this in their own way, as Eskimos, Aleuts, and Indians. To continue to assimilate them, to continue to keep them as pets unable to care for themselves, to continue to attempt to remake them into anything else but what they are, is to commit slow cultural genocide.

As for the state of Alaska, it must realize that Native people are not its enemies, seeking to undermine it; they are in fact the state's first citizens who never went to war against the immigrants who later settled here but rather accepted them with open arms. Neither are the resources of the state threatened by Alaska Natives who to this day have managed to conserve those natural resources. The state must, by constitutional amendment, accept the existence of Eskimos, Aleuts, and Indians and accept the fact that their needs are not the same as the needs of immigrants from other states and countries.

Relations are sad between the state and its first citizens who gave up much so that they could exist together. Certainly this can change. The state must play a role in helping its first citizens back to health.

The Alaska Federation of Natives
The Alaska Federation of Natives (AFN) was established to halt the loss of Native land to federal, state, and private parties, and to acquire title to lands owned by Native people on the basis of aboriginal land rights. Now the AFN must turn to seeking redress for other equally important inheritances of Native people, inheritances that were lost because the basis for holding them was slowly eroded by detrimental laws and adverse decisions in federal and state courts.

The AFN must realize that Native people have given up all they can give up; there is nothing left to give up in compromise any more. The federation must halt any further erosion of the inherited

rights of village people. In fact they must begin again to seek
redress and the reinstatement of rights already lost.

Specifically, AFN must return to Congress, not to amend the land
settlement it successfully fought for, but rather to settle the other
equally important claims of their people:

1. the right to self government,

2. the right to establish ordinances,

3. the right to enforce the ordinances,

4. the right to establish courts,

5. the right to hunt and fish for subsistence without
   interference by state law,

6. the right to use subsistence resources like salmon and other
   game on their lands and waters for commercial purposes so
   as to end economic dependence on state and federal welfare
   programs, and

7. the right to tax exemptions on their properties and holdings
   which are exemptions now enjoyed by other Native peoples
   of this country.

These rights are inherent to Alaska's Native people and they were
never voluntarily given up by them. In fact, they were taken away
without their knowledge and without their approval. They were
stolen. The tribes which together comprise the federation, for the
good of their people, for their very survival, must now turn in
earnest to recovering their rights. They must do this now while the
elders who survived the Great Death and their children are still
with us.

To argue their case for redress they do not need lawyers. Their
case is simple and compelling. They would not be asking for more
money or more programs. Neither would they be asking for
something which they did not need, or something that someone
else could give them or do for them. They would only be asking to
be themselves again, to run their own lives again, to pick up the
struggle for life again.

Since the turn of the century, they have been ruled by others,
trustingly, patiently, quietly. Because of the trauma of disease and

the collapse of their world, they have quietly allowed this to happen. And, for a time, it may have been good that there was someone there to help them replace the system that had collapsed around them. But that time has gone on too long. It is time for the survivors of the Old World to pick up the struggle for life again. The system they are living in now is killing them, the way they are living now is killing them, further depressing an already depressed soul.

Alaska Native villages and people are indeed depressed. Not only are we suffering spiritually as a result of seemingly forgotten assaults to our psyche, but this psychological depression is exacerbated by the possibility of total dependence on handouts from federal and state governments. From birth to death many Alaska Natives are cared for by government. Many of us hold high-school diplomas but are unemployed. Our families, living on government dole, do not need each other for support. Too often, we feel useless and have nothing to do.

This almost total dependence on others further undermines the already depressed spirit of many Native people. And the only way it can end is if we take back the responsibility of feeding, clothing, and housing our people; indeed, take back responsibility for all aspects of our physical and spiritual lives. Only then can we pick up once again the struggles of life.

This opportunity to pick up the struggles of life is what the AFN and its member villages must fight for. To some, the seven rights we have to regain mean sovereignty. To the Alaska Natives in the villages, these rights mean life, real life, with hard work, sweat, and no time to feel sorry for ourselves.

Native villages and Native people who seek to regain the seven rights are not asking for something new, something we never held before. We seek the opportunity to live not only the way our forebears lived, but to regain responsibilities now held by federal and state governments. These responsibilities belong to us. We want to be normal again. The way many of us live now is abnormal, like caged animals. We are fed, housed, watered, cared for, but we are not free, and it is killing us.

This is what the Alaska Federation of Natives can and should do. The time of giving up things is over. There is nothing left to give away. There is nothing left with which to negotiate. The AFN and its village people are against the wall. There is no more room for retreat. If the AFN wishes to help its village people back to health, it has to finish the job that only started with the Alaska Native Claims Settlement Act. We must secure the seven rights that are basic to the continued survival and soul of Alaska Native people, rights that mass death through disease and trauma took away from us.

Alaska Native people are ready to reassume these rights and responsibilities; without them, we will cease to exist as a people. It is not a matter of semantics or politics; it is a matter of survival.

Closing

I do not know if anyone will understand or agree with what I have written. Nor do I know that if it is understood, the recommendations will be followed. But I am convinced that what I have written is the truth and will be supported by facts. What I have written is the summary of five years' work, sometimes frustrating and anguishing work, but work nonetheless. It did not come to me in one flash, rather it came in bits and pieces. But finally the pieces fit, so I wrote them down for others to read.

Certainly there are others more qualified and more respected than I who could probably compose a more perfect letter. But this letter is from the heart and is born out of my own suffering and imprisonment. In suffering and imprisonment, I have found, life becomes starkly clearer, shed of the noise and the static of the world.

Yet I did not withdraw from the only world I have ever known, the world of my childhood and the world in which I struggled with seemingly insignificant results. No, while I might have been five years in prison, I have never left my village, nor my own Yup'ik people. In fact I return to them in spirit. While missing out on the seemingly good aspects of the life of my village and people, I certainly have not been spared their sorrows and their own suffering. These I have shared with them fully, sorrowing with them, seeking all the harder in our collective soul for answers.

At times I have felt like giving up. Sometimes things look hopeless. But from the Apostle Paul I have been trying to learn to be content in whatever state I am in. I now see those things that brought me—and still bring so many of my brothers and sisters—to alcohol abuse and alcoholism. So now, when I see them, their suffering, their unhappiness, I see my old self and try all the harder to lead them to the truth, the truth that freed me even as I sat in this prison, the same truth that can free all Native people who have become prisoners of the unhappiness born of the evil of the Great Death and the subsequent trauma which it fathered.

This letter that I have written is a part of that truth, the truth which was hidden from me by my previous life, by my own stubbornness, pride, unvented emotions, and my addiction to alcohol, which momentarily eased the suffering these bring.

This letter is not from a wise man, because were I wise I would not be where I am. This letter is from a man who learned only from suffering, the lessons literally beaten into his soul. But for this I am grateful, for now I have finally seen what was before my very eyes from the time I was a child. So I share what I have learned—been taught—in hope that the tragedy which engulfed my life and that of my family and villages may never happen again.

I will close by saying that I, once the most hopeless of men, no longer am without hope. I now live in hope. I also have faith that The One who started this good work in us by creating us will complete it.

Yuuyaraq: A Commentary

Walter Soboleff
Tenakee Springs, Alaska

As Alaska Native people tried to deal with the demands of the American school system and the dominant society, there emerged a few individuals, such as Harold Napoleon, upon whom their peers cast a mantle of leadership. The new "hunting ground" was full of new dangers, in the face of which some of these leaders gave their utmost at great personal sacrifice and at the expense of their family lives. Communities were not always aware of the many pressures associated with serving in leadership roles in this new world, with the result that the persons "up front" often stumbled and sometimes literally died. As we are now coming to understand, our leaders must face many storms and the people back home must be supportive and must share their counsel and encouragement. And we have to remember that our elders are also still leaders. We must be a team.

In his highly motivated and soul-searching essay, prompted in part by his experiences as one of our Native leaders, Harold discusses some of the causes of alcoholism and alcohol abuse among this generation of Alaska Native people. It is a story of a people who once enjoyed their land in peace, living a subsistence lifestyle and sharing a spiritual relationship with the land.

Harold discusses the death by disease of almost a whole generation of Natives, and he notes that currently there is another wave of destruction due to alcoholism and drug abuse. To combat this destruction, Harold mentions the importance of the spirit world, without which the people lose not one but many battles.

Without this spiritual base, all other ambitions become as piles of wood, unused and finally lost.

The struggles of Alaska Natives are not over, and this article may well assist youth and older folk in realizing the importance of traditional Native strengths as valuable tools in times of adjustment. The determination of our ancestors made it possible for us to survive as a people up until today. To continue, we must recover and build upon the many virtues which did not die with the last generation.

My appreciation to Harold Napoleon must be expressed here as he rose above the prison walls to overcome his troubles, much as his ancestors overcame theirs. Their determination, courage, sacrifice, patience, and faith have not died but are alive in each of us.

Our thanks to Harold who arose to share his good spirit with us.

Commentary on Harold Napoleon's Paper

Oscar Kawagley
First Nations House of Learning
University of British Columbia

In my early years I was raised by my grandmother, a very wise woman who survived the Great Death. According to her, my father died of injuries incurred during a drinking binge. While growing up, I used to find her crying by herself, and to my query of "Why are you crying?" she would say, "Oh, poor me, I am just crying for no particular reason except for the many that departed." This was said as if she was chastising herself and apologizing for this very important emotional outlet. Reflecting now, I am sure that she was crying not only for her beloved daughter who had died during that time, but also for the many others she had known who had passed away as well. She never took the time to explain why it was that, in that instant, she was so sad.

But it is that "Why?" that permeates all my being, as it probably does with many other Yupiaq people. And the answers to the Whys? in everyday reality are important, because they give us ways to define who we are and the wisdom to navigate a life that has meaning. I believe the emotional consequences of receiving no answers when we ask Why? are among the reasons our Yupiaq people are losing their values and traditions. I think Harold answers this Why? very well: it is the great loss of loved ones and, above all, the loss of the shamans, the spiritual leaders, that caused the Yupiaq hegemony to slip away from a traumatized people. It is a deep-seated grief that has not been acknowledged or resolved. It is a traumatizing experience which has been ignored and thus never brought to closure.

In Yupiaq being, the three realms of the human, the natural, and the spiritual are inseparable. The Spirit of the Universe conceived and made the heavens and the earth and continues to flow through all our constructs. The traditional Yupiaq acknowledged this through their rituals and ceremonies that were created to maintain and sustain balance between the three worlds. It brings into mind one of the most important ceremonies of the Yupiaq, the Feast of the Dead. This ceremony was done yearly in alternating villages to pay tribute to those who had traveled to the spiritual world during that year. The young who had been given the names of departed travelers were acknowledged by their family members with gifts of new clothing and/or choice portions of food. This ceremony brought to a close the event of people's physical departure from their communities.

To give up something so sacred as the Feast of the Dead and related values and traditions had to be deeply traumatic. The new religions, being cut off from nature, provide no adequate substitute to most Yupiaq, including myself. The Yupiaq cathedrals were wherever they happened to be, and their spirituality was more than a weekend religion in a building built specifically for that purpose.

The traditional Yupiaq house was one with nature. Now, when I look at the new houses built up off the ground on pilings, I think to myself, "These houses are not of our (Yupiaq) design, and the people living in them are not even in touch with nature; they are above nature, just as the modern world sees itself to be above nature." The further away one gets from nature, the easier it is to lose respect and politeness toward all things. This respect for nature must be restored, because through it flows the giver-of-life, the spirit. Social mayhem is wrought in our modern Native villages as we depart farther and farther from nature. Talking Circles, as Harold proposes, will do much to bring out these latent feelings. However, I think the villages, and churches as well, need to conduct traditional ceremonies and services, perhaps in a modified form, that specifically address the Great Death losses, where remembrances and feelings can be freely expressed and shared with all.

It must not end there. We must look at the pseudo-realities being built around television, especially violence to oneself and others, including women and children. New wants and needs are introduced and often these new things are inappropriate to our culture and ecological systems. Yet, we readily accept them because they seemingly make our work easier. However, connected to these are high costs to us as Yupiaq, and to our environment and our spirit. We have many values, customs and traditions that are still workable today, and we need to build these into the infrastructure of the world we want. This will determine whether we, as Yupiaq, remain viable or not. We must juxtapose the modern world with what ours used to be.

The institutions of the modern world are slowly eroding and strangling the planet. Materialism, in the Yupiaq world, used to be insignificant, but now we need more and more money to meet the advertisement-induced wants and supposed needs of our families. The flashing lights of new technological gadgets and tools constantly bombard us, but we don't seem to be experienced enough, either in our Yupiaq ways or in the modern world's ways, to be sensitive to their destructive impact upon our existence as a people. We must begin to reconstruct the world as we want it to be, through self-education and self-determination. Harold has shown us how we can begin the journey. *Quyana!*

Impressions of Yuuyaraq
from a Chevak Resident's Point of View

John Pingayak
Cultural Heritage Director
Cup'ik Cultural Heritage Project
Kashunamiut School District
Chevak, Alaska

There are usually several points of view regarding any hypothesis, but considering what I have learned from my elders, I have come to believe that Harold's theory is absolutely true. Various colleagues and friends have also read the paper and they agree.

I would like to offer several points to support and comment about Harold's ideas.

Cangarlagpiik Epidemics
Two elders, who have recently passed away, confirmed that there were two epidemics, called *cangerliigpiit* in Cup'ik [the Chevak way of saying Yu'pik], that devastated our people. The two elders said many of the villages were wiped out. Some of the villages that used to exist along the Black River no longer exist today. After the epidemic, one household with children looked like they were sleeping. Some households were forced to bury all of their family members. If this type of devastating incident happened today it would be considered traumatic for the people who experienced it. It is likely that our ancestors may not have recovered from this experience and that the effects were passed on from generation to generation. Many of our innocent youth must have wondered what their grandparents were crying about. During my time, my mom cried about the hardships she had gone through, and some of those incidents are still clear in my mind. I

have no doubt that what happened to my parents affects my life in some way or another today.

How Our People Were Treated by the Missionaries

Many of the students who attended mission schools feel that parts of their lives were taken away. Many of our people were made to feel that they were bad or made to feel guilty about who they were. We often thought that the first teachers and missionaries were superior to us. During confession, many created "sins" that they had not committed at all. And the negative opinions that some missionaries held about our people are recorded in numerous documents.

Fortunately, things are changing. Today we are slowly getting back to our own values and cultural beliefs. And we are coming to understand that the beliefs and values held by our ancestors were not all that different from those of the Christian religions.

Constant Pressure and Opposition from the Outside World

Rapid changes forced upon us by the western culture have also introduced a lot of stress and uncertainty into many of our people's lives. The subsistence and trapping economy was changed overnight into a cash economy. Many of our parents were forced to find jobs to survive, and most of those jobs were menial labor and other low class positions.

Today, the trend is changing little by little. Some of our people are graduating from college and taking prominent jobs. However, we still have a long way to go.

Many outside forces are shaping the villages and the Native people of today. Some of these forces are introduced through the Western form of government at both the federal and state levels. One recent example is the various subsistence laws which seem to confront Natives with a losing battle. At times, the frustration of our Native people is unbearable, but we need to be united in order to succeed as a people. And we need to be involved in the law-making process.

Many of the problems that Native communities face require money and lobbying efforts by our people. Some of those problems are alcohol and drug abuse, social problems such as suicide and rape, health problems such as inadequate trash and solid waste control, inadequate housing, lack of jobs in the villages, young people failing and dropping out of schools, and lack of natural resources and other economic development options to make us independent.

Philosophies and Native Cultural Ways of Life Not Fully Accepted by Mainstream Society

Although self-determination has been effective, the needs and expectations that Native communities have in regard to the educational system have not been fully realized. Many villages have expressed interest in reviving cultural heritage activities and Native language use in their schools, because it has become evident that practicing one's cultural heritage and speaking one's heritage language promotes self-esteem in young people. In meetings such as Elders' Conferences, young people have themselves expressed similar interests. Nevertheless, bureaucratic red tape has too often limited the efforts of these communities and young people. Schools must come to understand their obligation to include these courses and activities because some of our young people end up living in the villages and we cannot afford to alienate them from their own environment. If children are not taught their Native ways, they will tend to feel helpless in their home environment. This lack of self-dependence may lead to alcohol and drug abuse. These are a few of my concerns about the things that contribute to our state of being. Many of these can be avoided if they are dealt with at the village level. Some of the suggestions and possible solutions that Harold mentioned would be helpful in such a village-level approach. For example, talking about what happened in the past will require special settings such as Chevak's "Sod Houses" or the Old Minto Camp. These Native-style settings for healing protect the integrity of personal feelings and emotions.

Thank you for giving me the time to comment on Harold's paper which is very personal for me as well as for our Native people of Alaska.

Yuuyaraq: A Commentary

Joe Slats
College of Rural Alaska
University of Alaska Fairbanks

I invited Harold Napoleon to my Education 101 class on November 3, 1990, to speak more in depth about his paper, "The Way of the Human Being." For many of the students, his talk hit very close to home and family. Some students became emotional as they remembered personal experiences or incidents that occurred within their villages.

Older students, who are not in my class, have told me how powerful they feel Harold's paper is. Some of them mentioned that Harold could have been writing about their lives. Both the paper and the talk gave some individuals more determination to do better, for themselves and for other Native people. I have discussed "The Way of the Human Being" in a number of classes and although the response varied, the most frequent comment concerned how powerful the paper is.

In today's understanding, some of the topics that Harold brings up are foreign even to Native people. For example, Harold discusses the old culture. Unless one does more research on the old culture, this aspect of the paper may be hard to comprehend. We believe that we are practicing our culture now, and that we are doing what we have done for hundreds and hundreds of years. However, further research shows that the old culture that Harold refers to is much different than the one we are accustomed to. The beliefs, traditions, and hardships that our forebears experienced are almost beyond our imagination today.

Many of Harold's ideas make sense and may help explain some of what Natives have become today. Some communities are trying to take control of their lives through the implementation of self-government, which will enable them, among other things, to control the importation of alcohol and/or drugs. While this ban serves as a deterrent for individuals with addiction problems, some communities still have severe problems with alcohol and drugs.

Although not all Native people have substance abuse problems, it affects every one of us, and in this regard, *Yuuyaraq* has something of value to offer. Dry villages have attempted to take some measure of control over the abuse of alcohol and drugs, but banning importation by itself does not address the heart of the matter. Harold's paper focuses on why Native people are prone to these problems in the first place. He speaks of a confused, lost people trying to fill an empty space that they are not even aware of. Some of the symptoms of this confusion are substance abuse, child abuse, suicide, and domestic violence. The way to begin to heal this pain is through honest communication and understanding of our past. It is an avenue to pursue in helping our Native people realize what is going on in our lives.

After being a foster parent for a year and a half and working at the university for two years, I am finding out more about what is going on in Native communities throughout the state. It is disheartening to hear about crimes against children, about the growing number of children with fetal alcohol syndrome or fetal alcohol effects, about students who experiment with alcohol and/or drugs, about suicide attempts, and about growing discipline problems. It is imperative that we start on the path of becoming whole people again while we still have a future. How long can a people last when a large percentage of their young adults have substance abuse problems or are likely to commit suicide, and when so many babies are born already damaged or are damaged by abuse while still infants?

If the suggestions Harold offers are to work effectively, they must be made available at the village level. And if municipal and traditional governments decide to take on the responsibility of implementing Harold's suggestions, they must also give up certain money-making activities. Bingo is one of the activities that

I believe is pulling families further apart. For a village to take on a healing responsibility, it must not only think about the type of program that will be effective for the village residents, but also about other village-supported activities that will either support or detract from the healing program. School districts must also think about their role in the healing process and how they can incorporate it into their curricula.

Harold's manner is soft-spoken, and he is calm as he addresses the pain and suffering of his people. However, that does not detract from the urgency of his message. He states that we are still burying our people, a fact that every one of us who has lived in a village has experienced personally. He also stresses that there is hope for Natives to become again the strong and proud people that it is our heritage to be. Each one of us has a responsibility to contribute to that goal.

A Response to Harold Napoleon's Paper "*Yuuyaraq:* The Way of the Human Being"

Maynard E. Gilgen
Department of Psychology
University of Waikato
Hamilton
Aotearoa, New Zealand

Tena koe te Rangatira Harold Napoleon

He mihi atu kia koe

Ki te tautoko nga mahi, nga whanaunga, kua koorero,

"*Yuuyaraq:* The Way of the Human Being."

Your words have moved me to express my support, understanding, experience, and love to you, your family, and your people. I commend you on the way you have articulated and integrated your personal experiences with those of your family and your tribe.

You write, "I do not know if anyone will understand or agree with what I have just written." Speaking for and on behalf of my family and myself, I recognize that your journey has been very similar to the path of my ancestors. We Maaori, the indigenous people of Aotearoa, have journeyed down the road of abuse, violence, and attempted cultural genocide in all the forms experienced by you and your people.

I am 30 years old and come from a mixed marriage, my mother being Maaori (sub-tribe, Ngati Tahinga; tribe, Tainui) and my dad,

Swiss (place of origin, Wahlern; canton, De Berne). I will respond to your paper from the perspective of my mother's people.

There are many similarities between your people's experiences and mine: a disproportionate over-representation in the prisons, abhorrent statistics regarding disease and health issues, dismal failure in the education system, and the highest ratio of unemployed people in our country. There are also some interesting differences.

One difference is the timing and process of colonization. I believe that your people are now where my ancestors were at the turn of the century when there was a general belief that the Maaori people were going to die out. Like Alaska Natives, my ancestors were traumatized by a Great Death, a period in which Maaori culture was attacked physically, spiritually, and culturally through disease, land confiscation, inter-tribal warfare, and the introduction of alcohol and non-indigenous religions. To deal with the rape of our land and culture, we also used a range of coping mechanisms that included self-blame, alcohol abuse, violence amongst ourselves, depression, suicide, and denial.

Thanks to the hope, vision, faith, endurance, and determination of our ancestors who passed on and the elders who are with us today, we survived the legacy of violence and abuse to come back from near-death. Today, our numbers continue to increase to where we are 12 percent of the population of Aotearoa, and our customs, traditions, language, and spiritual beliefs are experiencing a renaissance.

However, there is still much work to be done. For example, it is not uncommon for Maaori people of my generation to be unable to speak our native language. This is a result of the colonizing process. My mother's generation, similar to your people, were physically beaten for speaking their native tongue at school. Thus, our parents and extended families encouraged my generation to work hard and succeed within *Tauiwi* (non-Maaori) schools and universities, and not to concern ourselves with our language or culture. This has proven successful for only a minority of our people.

Today, the "ideal" of integration is being surpassed and replaced with Maaori-based schools for our children. *Te Kohanga Reo* (literally, "language nests") for pre-school children and *Kura Kaupapa Maaori* (Maaori-based schools) for children 5 to 12 years old both focus on the Maaori experience. Maaori high schools for 13- to 17-year-old students are currently being developed. These initiatives were implemented in the 1980s as a response by Maaori people to the imminent death of our language and culture.

I am currently completing an M.A. and diploma in clinical psychology at local universities. However, it has been through working with my people in the community that I have gained an understanding of our history and why we are where we are today. Hence, I have personally worked towards developing my mother's language and culture and, along with other Maaori community workers and university graduates, I have struggled to challenge those current Western-based programs and interventions that are inappropriate for our people.

One way we have begun tackling these issues is through the development of Maaori-based non-violence programs. These programs are designed to help Maaori explore culturally appropriate alternatives to violence. Since its inception three years ago, I have been a counselor and supervisor in one such program, *Te Whanau Rangimarie O Taamaki Makaurau* (People for Peace and Non-Violence, based in the Auckland area and called TWR). The founding members of TWR have been working to stop violence and inter-personal abuse in our community and tribe for the past twenty to thirty years.

TWR is a non-profit organization which has been developed by Maaori volunteer community workers to assist Maaori offenders or victims of violence. The program has replaced Western interventions that have proven to be inappropriate and ineffective for our people. Domestic violence and sexual abuse are the main areas of concern, although drug and alcohol abuse and unemployment are often intertwined with these.

I agree with your perspective on the issues you raise in your paper and I strongly support your recommendations and suggestions for healing this living trauma. Your Talking Circles, similar to our *hui*, are an appropriate way to begin the healing process for individuals, families, sub-tribes, tribes, and nations. *Hui* has been one of the many cultural practices our ancestors have maintained and passed on to us. For centuries we have used *hui* to prepare for coming events, for healing, for education and training, and for enjoyment and celebration. It is through this process that TWR programs have been developed, evaluated, and refined.

In line with traditional Maaori beliefs and values, our approach is holistic and includes the entire family. There is a support group for women and children who have been abused, and a non-violence group for men who are either abusers or victims of violence.

There are three sub-groups for men that operate simultaneously. The first group serves as an orientation for men referred to us by the courts and agencies, or who have come to us voluntarily. The second group is a closed, twelve week non-violence program. The third group serves those who have overcome their violent patterns and wish to put something back into the program by becoming trained facilitators and counsellors.

Further plans for the Maaori men's group include the design and development of Talking Circles for those who have been victims of abuse and the initiation of a group specifically for male Maaori sexual abusers.

We believe in culturally oriented and gender appropriate counseling. For example, in counseling couples or families, we always have both a woman and a man counsellor facilitate the process. This ensures greater accountability to each other. It has also enabled us to monitor both ourselves and the people with whom we work.

Currently, we have a women and children's safe-house. We are also in the process of acquiring a men's house that will allow abusive or violent men to receive help in a residential facility so that the women and children who are their victims can remain safe in their home environment.

TWR is based in the southern region of Auckland, the largest city in Aotearoa. Although we work within our geographical tribal area, we also serve anyone in need of help, including members of other tribes and ethnic backgrounds.

Recently, we initiated a non-violence program in another region of our tribe. Our aim, as one *kaumatua* (elder) expressed it, is to build

Talking Circles on solid foundations that will ensure effective and lasting non-violence programs. Through such action we promote communication from the heart that leads to healing.

Members of TWR and other Maaori-based groups working toward improving the well-being and health of our people often assist in the redesign of government programs and policies. We also offer workshops, seminars, and lectures on non-violence for our local high schools, technical institutes, and various community groups and agencies.

On a larger scale, Maaori tribes have implemented various tribal interventions for health and well-being. For instance, in 1990 my tribe, Tainui, released the Tainui Health Plan outlining a plan of action through which the tribe will address health from a holistic perspective. The plan emphasizes the interrelationship between health and social, cultural, and economic aspects of development and identifies ways we can work in cooperation with the New Zealand Health Council. Although our people have been struggling to rectify injustices and abuse committed by the state for the last 150 years, this Tribal Health Plan in conjunction with government support is an exciting and encouraging initiative for our people.

The seven rights you discuss, Harold, are rights that must be of concern to Maaori and all indigenous people. The attainment of those rights is a vision toward which we are working. Burnout is common, so if this work is to progress we must consistently watch out for each other, and as you expressed, maintain honest communication amongst our own and others.

At the end of the day, the only way to genuinely heal our people is, as you expressed, for us to take responsibility for the design, development, and implementation of indigenous-based programs for the health and well-being of our own. There is no other way.

Ma to Atua Tamaiti ra ma te Wairua Tapu hoki Ratou Atua kotahi nei e whakapai koe, me to whanau, me to mahi.

Tena koe Harold Napoleon.

Response to
"Yuuyaraq: The Way of the Human Being"

Barbara Harrison
Research Fellow
Center for Maaori Studies and Research
University of Waikato
Hamilton, New Zealand

The purpose of my response is to compare and contrast my own observations of contemporary Yup'ik and New Zealand Maaori life in light of Harold's paper. I lived and worked in southwestern Alaska for about four years between 1977 and 1982 and have lived and worked in a Tainui Maaori community for about the same period of time. The indigenous peoples of these two areas of the world have much in common in the suffering which has resulted from contact with Euro-Americans.

When I first read Harold's paper, one point seemed to be critical in understanding the difference between Yup'ik and Maaori life today, and that point had to do with who was to blame for the problems both peoples have experienced. Harold indicated that the Yupiit [plural for Yup'ik] blamed themselves for the disasters which struck them. Although I am told that Maaori did blame themselves and their own culture in the past, the Maaori people that I know today do not blame themselves, they blame historical circumstances resulting from contact between Europeans and Maaori.

The Tainui tribal area, where I now live, was invaded by Europeans in 1863, and the tribal members who survived those wars lived in exile in another region of the country for twenty years before they were able to return to the small reserves of land which were all that remained to them of their once-productive farming region. Their population was decimated during the nineteenth and early twentieth centuries as the result of epidemics of European diseases, and whole communities disappeared as a result. The Maaori language experienced a dramatic decline following the introduction of "English only" policies in New Zealand schools. In 1900, 90 percent of Maaori children entered schools as speakers of the Maaori language. By 1960, only 26 percent of children spoke the language (Walker, 1990, p. 147).

The introduction of alcohol had disastrous consequences during the 1860s among Maaori of both the North and South Islands.

> By the late 1960s, Maaoris living in the areas most affected by land sales and confiscation were living in debt and confined to run-down reserves, poorly administered because of the confusion of multiple ownership brought about by the land courts. Already, South Island Maaoris had passed through a liquor craze in the mid-1960s which left them "squalid, miserable and lifeless," foreshadowing the fate of North Island tribes later in the decade. By now, new labour demands and continual loss of land were causing increasing mobility of the Maaori work force and a passion for drinking was sweeping though the North Island coastal communities. This upturn in drinking assisted in the breakdown of traditional leadership already well in progress because of land sales. In some communities, land sales gradually became the means for leaders and their kinfolk to get liquor, and liquor became the means by which both private and government land agents got land (Alcohol Research Unit, 1984, pp. 4–5).

Even a generation or two ago, I'm told, highly destructive drinking was common.

However, a Maaori revitalization began in the early years of the twentieth century. The Maaori population began to increase and in 1990 was estimated at 428,000, nearly ten times the number of the 1896 census. In the early 1900s, Sir Apirana Noata, the first Maaori university graduate, achieved political prominence and began to argue for opportunities for Maaori to develop their own land. He and Princess Te Puea Herangi encouraged and developed revivals of Maaori carving, song and dance during the first half of the twentieth century, and these revivals formed important components in the overall movement toward self-determination. In recent years, programs with the specific purpose of maintaining the Maaori language have been established in a wide range of settings including preschool, primary and secondary schools, universities, and in Maaori community centers. All in all, visitors to New Zealand today are impressed with the sense of "cultural energy" of contemporary Maaori life.[*]

One significant foundation of the Maaori revitalization has been the King Movement (*Kiingitanga*), centered in the Tainui tribal region of the North Island. This movement has surrounded the activities of the Maaori kings of the past and the present queen from the middle of the nineteenth century until the present. The King Movement provides both a political unifying force and a spiritual focus for its followers, and the unity and spirituality of the movement have contributed to the continuing adaptability of the Maaori people.

Alcohol, however, is still a problem today. In 1986, the Maaori admission rate for alcohol dependence or abuse was approximately double the non-Maaori rate, and I know from my experience in a Maaori community that young people die in alcohol-related accidents and middle-aged people die sooner than necessary because of alcohol-related disease. But I and others believe that the situation is improving, largely as the result of Maaori efforts to control the problem.

One means of control has been through the establishment of clubs for various Maaori functions (e.g., sports) where drinking occurs in restricted hours and within the community. Clubs can provide constructive social environments as well as the opportunity for extended family and other community members to intervene in violent or otherwise destructive situations and for them to "keep an eye" on children. Because the clubs are located within Maaori communities, potential conflicts with individuals from outside the community (including the police) are minimized.

In his response to Harold's paper, Maynard Gilgen has described another effort at addressing the problem. In a number of places

---

"Cultural energy" is a term used by John Collier, Jr., as the title of an exhibit of his photographs in 1984.

around the country, Maaori are organizing programs to help men and women to deal with problems in relationships which are often associated with alcohol abuse.

A third approach focuses on the development of a tribal health plan. The Tainui tribe is in the process of implementing a tribal health plan under the auspices of the Tainui Maaori Trust Board. This plan will eventually employ Maaori community health workers in nine sub-regional centers who will conduct programs of health promotion from a Maaori perspective. One component of the health promotion program will focus on alcohol education in schools, youth organization, and adult community groups.

There are any number of comparisons that might be made between Maaori and Yupiit perspectives as Harold described them. For example, Harold recommends the establishment of Talking Circles in Alaskan villages. My experience in New Zealand suggests that many Maaori will find this recommendation appealing. Many of the Maaori that I know are already good talkers. *Hui* (get-togethers to discuss issues and problems) are frequent and include everything from small gatherings to discuss family concerns to national live-ins involving several thousand people and lasting for several days.

But it now seems to me that there are two critical points of comparison. The first is time. Maaori encountered the destructive impact of European contact as well as the impact of massive importation of alcohol in the middle of the nineteenth century, roughly one hundred years before the same impacts were being widely felt in rural Alaska. Maaori were badly demoralized but eventually began a drive for self-determination which has resulted in revitalization and at least some improvement in the many problems they have faced. Now, Maaori people seem to me to look forward to continuing improvement as the result of their efforts. Harold's paper offers the hope that the Yupiit will pass through the present crisis and will enter into their own revitalization in their own time.

This brings the discussion to what I see as the second critical point of comparison—the desire for self-determination that is widespread among both peoples. The Maaori revival is closely linked to Maaori determination to take control of their lives—

problems as well as solutions. Most have stopped blaming themselves for the social problems of the twentieth century and are demanding authority to take responsibility for finding solutions to the problems that developed when control over their own destiny was lost. There is every reason to believe that, for both Yupiit and Maaori, future survival and well-being is closely linked to the return of rights and responsibilities long denied them.

References cited

Alcohol Research Unit (1984). *Alcohol and the Maaori People.* Auckland: Alcohol Research Unit.

Walker, Ranginui (1990). *Ka Whawhai Tonu Matou: Struggle Without End.* Auckland: Penguin Books.

Yuuyaraq: A Commentary

David West
Rural Human Services Program
University of Alaska Fairbanks

My name is David West and I have been an external liaison with
the Native Culture Awareness class at Fairbanks Correctional
Center (FCC) for the past eight years. I have been and am
currently a member of the Prison Outreach Ministries for the State
of Alaska. I have been previously employed by both the Fairbanks
Native Association and the Tanana Chiefs Conference as a
counselor in FCC for Native inmates.

I met Harold Napoleon in early 1985 when he first came to FCC. I
was working as an alcohol counselor utilizing Native group
facilitation in weekly Talking Circles. The group was open to all
inmates but was focused primarily toward Alaska Native and
American Indian inmates.

Most of what is talked about in the circle is considered confidential
and not to be spoken of outside of the circle to respect the privacy
of the participants. I have gained permission from Harold to share
this experience in the hope and with the prayer that doing so will
help others avoid the pain and suffering that followed as a
consequence of his mistakes and decisions.

In the Talking Circle, a symbol is selected by the group to
designate a speaker who has the right to talk, without
interruption, about whatever is on his heart and mind until he is
through. The symbol also serves as a reminder that we must speak
the truth before the One Who Created Us and that we must have
courage in speaking about our deepest feelings. The group is
seated in a circle to promote equality within the circle and to

remind us that no one is any greater than any another. No one is required to speak, but all are encouraged to share what they feel or want to say.

When Harold first entered the classroom where the Talking Circle was held, I was impressed by the obvious intelligence of the man. I could sense that his burden of sorrow was very deep and very real. Since I have made it a practice not to inquire of anyone what their sentence or crime is, I did not ask Harold either.

During the course of that first Circle, which is always opened with prayer for guidance, many things were shared by the participants. They shared their thoughts about why they were incarcerated, about influences in their lives, who they missed and were lonesome for, their problems concerning alcohol and drugs, and generally how they were feeling.

When the symbol came to Harold, all that he was able to do was to look at it; he was unable to speak. After some time, he passed the symbol on to the next person and remained with the group. This pattern continued for the next several weeks.

When Harold began to share his feelings, he told us that he felt every day as though he were crawling out from under the rock of his guilt and shame. He felt that the rock was crushing the life out of him and that he was only able to make it thorough each day by the grace of God. As time progressed into the first year of Harold's time at FCC, I became increasingly worried about him. His health was obviously deteriorating; he was growing thinner and becoming more withdrawn. I often sat and talked with Harold about the old healing ways of our peoples and how much faith in the creator was directed toward the success of the ceremonies and rituals that accompanied and facilitated those healing ways.

We prayed together with the other inmates each time we got together and there was always talk of how things used to be for our people and the great and wondrous ways that we had, and still have, to help us live in a happy and healthful way, in relation to all others and to all things of the nature we are part of. Harold, however, seemed to continue to deteriorate and we became deeply concerned. It seemed to those of us who were regular participants that we were losing him to his pain and sorrow, and that truly, the life was being crushed from him. We continued to ask him to sit

with us at the drum during Native culture meetings and to try
singing with us, as singing is a very good tension reliever and
soothing agent.

About a year and a half later, Harold walked into the room and
there was most certainly something about him that was changed.
It seemed as though he could not wait for the circle to begin; he sat
right next to the leader, so as to be the first to speak, and he had an
energy about him we had never seen. When he began to speak
about what it was that had brought him to jail, we all understood
that something had happened within him. He told us the whole
painful story and brought it right up to the classroom we were in.
Then he said, "Last night I had a spiritual, a religious, experience
in my room. I was forgiven by God and my son and I can work
now towards forgiving myself. I know that I will always carry the
burden of the rock of my responsibility, but it is no longer
crushing me."

That's where I saw Harold Napoleon begin the process of his own
healing journey. I have continued to walk that journey towards
wellness with him and I hope I have encouraged him in his efforts.
I honor his strength and honesty in accepting his part in the
tragedy and his courage in facing the sorrow and pain of speaking
about it. I applaud his sharing it in an attempt to help others avert
such tragedy.

In *Yuuyaraq*, written on behalf of his people, Harold's voice is
strong. It raises questions that have remained unanswered and
unaddressed for many years, as though the people themselves
were sleeping and unaware. It brings to the light of recognition
those pains, confusions, and angers that have lain hidden in the
dark of denial and dismissal within the minds, spirits, and
emotions of the people far too long.

I hope that whoever reads this may understand that when you see
someone touched by the healing grace of the Almighty, before
your eyes, you no longer have any doubt as to the truth of the
words of that one so touched. I have no doubt in the words or in
the works of Harold Napoleon since that day to this day, and I
look with faith towards the next day.

Thank you.